Edmund B. Willson

The Proclamation of Freedom

A sermon preached in the North church, Salem, January 4, 1863

Edmund B. Willson

The Proclamation of Freedom
A sermon preached in the North church, Salem, January 4, 1863

ISBN/EAN: 9783337087500

Printed in Europe, USA, Canada, Australia, Japan

Cover: Foto ©Lupo / pixelio.de

More available books at **www.hansebooks.com**

The Proclamation of Freedom.

A

SERMON

PREACHED IN THE

NORTH CHURCH,

SALEM,

JANUARY 4, 1863.

BY EDMUND B. WILLSON,

Minister of the Church.

Published by Request.

SALEM:

T. J. HUTCHINSON,......PRINTER.

1863.

The Proclamation of Freedom.

A

A SERMON

PREACHED IN THE

NORTH CHURCH,

SALEM,

JANUARY 4, 1863.

BY EDMUND B. WILLSON,

MINISTER OF THE CHURCH.

Published by Request.

SALEM:

T. J. HUTCHINSON,.......PRINTER.

1863.

NOTE. — The Preacher of the following Sermon sees one reason, and no more, for consenting to the printing of it : that it may prevent, or remove, any misapprehension of what the Sermon contained.

SERMON.

ACTS XX. 35.—IT IS MORE BLESSED TO GIVE THAN TO RECEIVE.

The apostle Paul tells us that these were words of Jesus. They are not found in the Evangelical histories, and were probably preserved by tradition. We know nothing of the time, or circumstances of their utterance. But they are characteristic of the Teacher. His life assumes their truth, and illustrates it every day, and his death sets it forth in the strongest light.

To *receive* is a blessing, if the thing received be good, and it be received rightly, and for what it is. But to *give* is *more* blessed.

In receiving, the direction of the thought is apt to be inward, towards self, centring attention on this *me*, who is enriched. In giving, it is the other way. Thought and desire flow in the opposite direction, leading out from this me,— who is likely to be too much remembered. In the one case the lines of motion all tend to one point, narrowing to a centre. In the other they go widening from centre to circumference. If there is a blessing in having the empty cup filled from the fountain, there is greater blessing in possessing the fountain which fills the cup,— and still flows for other cups afterwards.

He who receives is not necessarily blessed by it. He may not know how to make a blessing of what he receives. He may not be willing, if he does know how. If he stops what he receives at himself, and does not let it flow past him, that is, if his receiving do not end in giving, the treasure rusts and moulds in its napkin. The better part of the blessing begins, not with the gift coming to us, but with its going on to others from us.

Our ascription of praise goes up to Him, "who is over all, God blessed forever." "Blessed," and Giver of all. Receiving nothing. Receive he cannot, for with him is all fulness. A truth of heaven, this is true on the earth also, that "It is more blessed to give than to receive."

There are two parties to that great transaction which has signalized the past week and the advent of a new year. The one has given, the other received.

Of the gift itself we pause to say but a word. Words fail to describe it. By the common consent of the most advanced of peoples and of men, slavery is a condition above all to be dreaded; not to be endured, if escape from it can be achieved at any sacrifice, or any danger; worse than death. Liberty is accounted by general consent the chief of earthly blessings. When men speak lightly of the evil of slavery, or the good of freedom, it is other men's slavery or freedom that they mean : never their own.

In vain does the imagination try to take in, measure, and feel adequately, the act of solemn grandeur

which has transpired. It so surpasses all ordinary
events; it is so peculiar in character; it is so sweeping
in its consequences, both as to time and numbers,
that the human mind struggles with its conceptions
in vain, in the attempt to compass it. I take one
soul, one life; I try to make myself know, by think-
ing, what slavery is to one. I think of daily waking
to obey another man's will; of beginning my toil
and ending it when he says; of pursuing it daily
where he says, and as long as he says; and with no
hope of reward, other than what he may please to
dole out in the food and clothing that shall keep me
able to work for him; of being thus daily robbed of
my time, my skill, the fruits of my industry, the fruits
of my thoughts. I think of this, not as a day's misery,
but as a life-long condition; not my condition only,
but that to which my children are doomed, and their
children; on forever; a doom without hope. I think
of this mastership not restricted to the wise and just,
but open to the worst: the passionate, the intemper-
ate, the profligate, the cruel, the avaricious.

I look at my children, and try to think what life
would be, if there were those who could come any
hour between me and them and say: " These are mine,
not yours. You are their father, but I am their owner.
Though you love them, and I do not pretend any
other than a pecuniary interest in them, I shall take
them from you; you will see them no more; you
must live without them; you cannot know their fate;
they are to be dead to you henceforth."

I try to think of these things in order to bring them

home to myself as reality. And when I do bring them home, my blood flows to my heart, and my soul freezes with horror.

But you say I must not suppose that slavery is felt by all as the degradation and wrong that it would be to me; nor that liberty is prized by all as the great blessing which I esteem it to be. If this were true it would confess worse of slavery than I have charged : that it unmakes the manhood of man ; turns his thought, and soul, and free will out of him, and leaves him a crushed brute. But if it does this sometimes, it does it *not every time;* for many as we know have so felt slavery, that they have sought to escape it at the risk of scourging, branding, iron collars and iron fetters, bloodhounds, bullets, separation from kindred, death.

To be brief,— Ownership ! The ownership of a man by a man ! That is Slavery. What can one say after that ? That you may not miss the point, you are to imagine yourself the owned, and to have no choice of owners.

Then I try to think what deliverance from such a condition would be : the gift of freedom to the enslaved. Is there any earthly gift to be named comparable to it ?

Then I pass from imagining the emancipation of one, and try to bring before me that of a family ; of a hundred ; of thousands ; of millions ! Of course I cannot do it. The mind cannot take it in. I do not exult at the spectacle before us, because I am awed by it.

Do not cavil at my speaking of the emancipation of millions as an accomplished fact. I do not forget that a word is but a word, and that it does not make slaves free to say they shall be free.

Nor do I forget that, when thirteen American colonies declared themselves independent of their mother government eighty-six years ago, that was only a declaration,— words. It did not make them independant to say that they were so. And yet it did. That was the end begun. The end was there in idea, in purpose, in inspiring hope. And after seven years' sacrifice, war, and suffering it was realized.

I do not know when these slaves of ten states declared free last Thursday, will *be* free ; nor how many will die without the sight. But though every one of them should die in slavery, the proclamation of freedom would be the same great solemn edict of justice, that shall be referred to through all history to the honor of this American people and its Government, and to the praise of God. I believe there is power in that word : tangible power, present efficiency. But if not there is moral power, which is superior to King-craft and State-craft, to generalship and gunnery ; and that word shall outshine all else that has been done in this war. In fact it is that which this proclamation stands for, which gives the war all the honor, or the excuse, it has. If this war is not a war for justice, a war for the preservation of liberty and the right of self-government, there is no excuse for it. And that is what this proclamation means ; only it extends the liberty and the right of self-government to a class who never before had either.

But if you are of those who have looked with alarm or objection to this step, you will possibly inquire, (as some have,) if this is after all, or if it so much as professes to be, an act of *justice;* if it is not justified purely on the ground of military necessity.

It is to be justified on both grounds. This act, like most human actions, is the product not of one but of many motives. Where many join in one act the motives to it are differently mixed in different minds. Some do not feel at all a motive which others feel strongly; while still others are controlled by a mingling of various considerations, which though distinct weigh together.

It has always been just that the slaves should have their liberty. But no power had been lodged with the government by its constitution to do them this justice, till Rebellion, by making war upon the Constitution and the nation in Slavery's behalf, gave the government this right; and, what was more, made it appear an imperative necessity to use it, as the only sure and effective way of saving itself, and saving the country, and perpetuating the national life and integrity. Then military necessity and justice came to have ends in common, attainable by common means. And from *both* the fiat came : — Let Slavery cease! Even military necessity would have had no right to do what is manifestly and grossly unjust. In spite of the proverb, that necessity knows no law, necessity does know many laws. If I could only preserve my life by sacrificing all the people of this city, even my necessity would not justify so great a crime. Necessity

itself declares that these many must be saved though
I perish. If the liberation of the slaves had been
a great act of *in*justice, falling on millions, and involv-
ing the innocent in ruin, it might not have been de-
fensible to have used such means, even to save the
country. Military necessity itself acknowledges that
there are injuries which must not be inflicted even
upon enemies, whatever advantages can be secured
thereby.

And perhaps it will be asked if this is not just
such a case. Some take that view of it, supposing
that the Government has invited insurrection, rapine,
murder. This however seems to me a wholly gratui-
tous assumption. The danger of insurrection will
come, if at all, through the action of the slave-holders. And with them, I sincerely believe, is the power
to prevent it. If the slave-holders make no opposi-
tion to the President's proclamation there will be no
insurrection. They know whether insurrection is to
be feared. And they know how the electricity can
be drawn harmlessly from that cloud, if there is any
in it. Frequently they say there is no such danger:
that the proclamation is but a dead letter, wholly my-
gatory. More often, however, they express fear.
There is a way of avoiding all danger. Let them
grant to their slaves the freedom which is theirs, and
offer to hire them at fair wages, and all danger of insurrection will vanish. Do you say that we cannot
expect them to do that? Then I say, they must not
expect us to sympathize with their fears of insurrection.

2

On the other hand; while military necessity alone
could not have sanctioned the proclamation of emancipation, the simple consideration of justice *alone*
could not govern in this question, if there had been
no military necessity to demand emancipation; for,
there are many things which justice requires to be
done, but which not every man may justly do. This
should be considered by those who blame the President for not declaring *every* slave free, at once,
throughout the land. The slaves of Missouri are as
unjustly held in bondage, as were those of Missis-
sippi. Justice as much requires their emancipation.
The President saw that plainly no doubt, but while
he saw that, and admitted it, he could not see that *he*
had any right to interfere where no imperative necessity demanded it.

If a man has assaulted another, it is clear that the
assailant deserves to be punished; but though it is
just that he should be fined or imprisoned, that does
not give me the right to make him a prisoner at my
own will, or to decide that he shall pay, and how
much.

The Italians may have rights, but the Emperor of
Russia has no right to interfere to enforce them.

The President in like manner cannot find that he
has the right to do, what is nevertheless right to be
done, emancipate the slaves of Maryland, Missouri,
Kentucky and Tennessee. Though where he felt that

he had not the right to emancipate by proclamation, he has nobly endeavored to bring about freedom by other means; means which, I trust, will prove successful at no distant day.

But what gives to this act of emancipation its great and permanent interest, and will make it memorable while the nation endures, or liberty has a home on the earth, is that it is an act of justice to an oppressed people.

Viewed simply as a military act designed to cripple an enemy, it is believed that it will have great effect. But so viewed it proves us neither great in wisdom, nor strong in right. All generals do what they can to cripple their enemies. There is nothing extraordinary in that. In that is nothing to accredit us with any higher quality than sagacity. But we have done two things in one in this emancipation. We have aimed a stroke of war policy at rebellion, and we have at the same time given back to millions of human beings rights which were *birth*-rights and inalienable, but of which they have been unjustly and cruelly robbed. It is this latter act of justice which is to live in history, and to make the first day of January, in the year of our Lord eighteen hundred and sixty-three, memorable.

Then let us turn from military necessity to justice. As Christians who lay no claim to knowledge of constitutional law, and who leave questions of military

necessity to those whose responsibility it is to decide
them, we go back to the simple fact that here are
millions of human beings who were slaves, now declared to be free. Here we discern an act of tardy
but glorious justice. We rejoice with these freed
people. It was just they should be free. Whatever
may be said of the part which any one has had in
effecting this result, the result is a righteous result.
It is one in which Christians cannot but feel a most
lively and rejoicing sympathy. It is no longer a war
policy we contemplate, but one of the fruits that holy
spirit, which Christ came to breathe into human souls.
It makes the gospel to *be* a gospel : good news.
He repeats again in our ears the words of the proph-
ecy,— and now with what weight of meaning! " The
Spirit of the Lord is upon me, because he hath an-
nointed me to preach the gospel to the poor. He
hath sent me to heal the broken-hearted ; to preach
deliverance to the captives, and recovering of sight to
the blind ; to set at liberty them that are bruised ;
to preach the acceptable of the Lord."

But if those who have received the inestimable
boon of freedom are blessed, yet more they who
have given it to them. The nation has risen from the
dust. Now may she lift up her head ; for, though
not yet is her warfare accomplished, she is bringing
forth fruits meet for repentance. She has clothed
herself invulnerably in the armor of righteousness.
It is worth all that it has cost us, and all that it will
cost, to have gained this strong position.

Nevertheless, this is not all that we have to do :— to sympathize and rejoice. Reconsider the text. It is more blessed to give than to receive. We have yet much to do to perfect this gift. The roots of slavery have struck deeper than we think. This fertile wrong has been the parent of one of the most cruel prejudices that ever perverted and abused the hearts of men. This prejudice is worse in the Northern states than in the Southern. It makes complexion a badge of degradation. It denies the dark skinned a home, or admittance to some states. It is as bad as slavery, every whit, in spirit. It is the same thing indeed as slavery. And those who feel it most and most express it, are the very material from which those hard-faced and flinty-hearted Northern drivers and masters of Southern slaves have been made, who are justly reputed the most remorseless of taskmasters and brutal of men. What more heathenish do we send missionaries to preach against in all the pagan coasts? Personal likes and dislikes may be treated with comparative patience. But the cowardly tyranny over weakness, that will make of a natural, God-appointed peculiarity of structure, or color, a ground of social proscription and outlawry, moves every chivalrous, not to say Christian sentiment in us to indignant protest. Men of the most revolting filthiness, of unclean lives, of foul and profane speech, whose breath sickens the pure, are often the very ones who with insult and abuse have followed these hunted, unprotected sheep through street, and car, and public hall; and they feel privileged to do it because better men encourage it; and even from churches, where the parable of the judgment is not expunged from the Bible, have these outcast people been banished. O, I have sometimes felt that some of us, who talk of slave-master's arrogance, may be no better than sanctimonious hypocrites; and we are no better, when we treat the black race, or any other of God's poor, and weak, and unfortunate ones with contempt and scorn, and still profess a regard for the teachings of the Son of God.

Under every dusky skin is a soul as much the care of God, as is his who issues proclamations from the Presidential seat, or his who folds a judge's robes about him, or his who sits at senate-boards, or his who ministers in lawn at the altar of religion. Why, is there a plain word in all the gospel, and is this equality of all souls before God not plainly written there? "My brother he is:" says Christ, pointing to the humblest, the captive, the hungry, the naked. "What you have done of kindness, or shown of love to him, I have received. What you have omitted of pitiful service or kindly regard to him in his misfortune, is an omission which falls upon me, and which I feel as my own."

It will take generations to abolish the effects of slavery, when slavery itself is done away. In one respect we have recognized the slave's manhood; it

remains to recognize it in other respects, in all re-
pects.

Freely we have received, let us freely give : it is
more blessed. In raising the fallen we shall be our-
selves lifted up. We have not yet begun to give.
It has cost little, comparatively, to speak a word.
Now, we must overcome prejudice. Now we must
show patience and forbearance, if those who have
long been oppressed are slow to forget the improvi-
dence, the carelessness, the unthrift which slavery
fosters. We must be considerate, if, intoxicated with
new-found liberty, they are for a while averse to labor,
and desirous to test to the full the new luxury of
idleness. They are a gentle people, by the consent of
all the witnesses. Treated kindly, they will be kind
and docile. Those who have been sometime free are
already manifesting an improvability, such as was not
to have been expected. They may not continue,
without interruption, to do so well. They will often
disappoint those who labor for them, and watch over
their condition. What then? All we can do for
them will be but light reparation for the wrongs which
have been done to their people by our people ; and were
it tenfold more, be it remembered that it is after all
more blessed to give than to receive.

Let us accept the proclamation of freedom to the
slave in the religious spirit in which it is concluded.
While we would invoke " the considerate judgment

of mankind," and especially the grateful, thoughtful
and merciful reflection of the Christian world, we
would invoke also " the gracious favor of Almighty
God !"

" O HOLY FATHER ! just and true
    Are all thy works and words and ways,
And unto thee alone are due,
    Thanksgiving and eternal praise !
As children of Thy gracious care,
    We veil the eye — we bend the knee,
With broken words of praise and prayer,
    Father and God, we come to Thee.
  * * * * *
Speed on Thy work, Lord God of Hosts !
    And when the bondman's chain is riven,
And swells from all our guilty coasts,
    The anthem of the free to Heaven,
Oh, not to those whom Thou hast led,
    As with Thy cloud and fire before,
But unto Thee, in fear and dread,
    Be praise and glory ever more."